Rob Temple is a journalist and founder of the @soverybritish Twitter account. Born in Peterborough, he now lives in Cambridge, takes two sugars and has lost every umbrella he has ever owned within three minutes of purchase.

Also by Rob Temple

Very British Problems

To Rhiain

CONTENTS

INTRODUCTION

Oh, hello. Sorry, I wasn't expecting you, but do come in and please take a seat. Now, let's not sugar-coat it, since we last spoke there's been good news and (a lot) of bad news. Let's get the bad news out of the way first: the Very British Problems epidemic hasn't just continued to sweep the nation, it's gone global. The good news: the kettle still works.

Our first sighting of the highly contagious condition known as 'Very British Problems' was published in 2013, examining the many strange and complicated symptoms demonstrated by the British within our own shores: in shops, restaurants, pubs, offices, bedrooms, planes, trains and automobiles and everywhere in between. Now, as we look back to that glorious, rose-tinted year from the bleak, grey abyss that is 2016, we can conclude that VBP has progressed rapidly in its severity; where once it was merely a sniffle, it is now a raging flu. And it shows no sign of abating.

To continue the documentation of the worldwide superbug that is VBP, we're going to study those sufferers, including you, who have taken VBPs around the planet, documenting their oddball behaviour from airport to beach, to mountain and back again (burned to a crisp, carrying a giant triangular chocolate bar and half a litre of ouzo).

We'll examine what we do well on our yearly two-week jaunts (championing sturdy footwear, orderly queueing, excessive drinking), what we do badly (relaxing, banana boats, other people) and everything else besides. We'll recall the nail-biting tales of those adventurers who dared to leave Britain and survived and we'll perfect the perfect kit-list if you so carelessly choose to travel abroad (in your condition! I mean, really?). If you *are* considerate enough to stay at home, we have plenty of notes within on the perfect Staycation, and we'll also give you a jargon buster for all those horrible words and phrases that come tied to travel.

Many of you will have arrived at this book via the @SoVeryBritish Twitter feed, which continues to grow (because let's face it, there's still plenty to moan about), now nearing 1.5 million of us searching for an insight into the complexities of the British psyche and our peculiar customs. (If you're not British but just a bit awkward, you'll probably like to join in too.)

Now, in this second volume of *Very British Problems*, as we look across the oceans, will we find an answer? Can we find a way to stop making things so calamitous for ourselves? No, probably not, to be honest . . . but at least it might be sunny.

There, managed to get through the whole of that without a single mention of the EU. Oh, bugger it . . .

Rob Temple, Cambridge, 2016

1. BOOKING AND PREPARATION

'Great, if that's where you want to go …' Translation: It won't be my fault when this holiday turns bad

Looking the busiest you've ever been at work because you've spent the week before your holiday booking restaurants and frantically researching water-slide parks

Making sure your house is the tidiest it's ever been for the two weeks of the year that you won't be in it

Working on your computer while standing up for ten minutes, to ease everyone into the fact that you're about to leave for two weeks

Trying to choose what to wear for work – having already packed all your best clothes – the pair of waterproof hiking trousers, the gigantic white dinner shirt or the T-shirt you won by drinking five pints of Guinness.

Booking a hotel purely on the basis that more than one review stated it provided a decent selection of fried goods for breakfast

Getting a flight for the bargain price of £6 (+£40 per person booking fee, +£50 per kilo of luggage, +£75 per seat, +£200 in taxes, +£20 for a special rucksack you don't realise you've purchased until it's delivered)

Spending a whole day typing
up a work handover document,
fully aware that it won't ever be
looked at, not even if you were
never seen again

Knowing you have more chance of finding
the Holy Grail, the meaning of life and a
specific pin in a giant stack of other pins
than of locating your travel adaptor and
mini padlock keys

'Look, I don't mind where we go'
Meaning 1: I don't mind where
we go. Meaning 2: I mind more
than anything I've ever minded
about ever (and there'd better be
water-slides)

Getting a pile of one dollar bills from the Bureau de Change and pretending you're a gangster for a bit

Saying '35 degrees in Spain!' every time someone mentions bad weather for a month leading up to your break

Checking the weather forecast and seeing that it'll actually be 36 degrees in Britain while you're away

Printing out every single reference and email and putting them in a plastic A4 documents wallet, despite having used your mobile to check in everywhere for the past five years

Emptying your Sky planner so you have enough room to record a fortnight's worth of *Pointless*, *The Chase* and *University Challenge*

Ringing your bank to let them know you're going abroad, to give yourself the opportunity to write a stiff letter when they inevitably block your card anyway

Booking a 'Top Secret Hotel' and hoping it doesn't turn out to be caravan in someone's driveway ... like last time

'Yep, great, see you in the meeting on Monday'
Translation: I keep telling you I'm on holiday as of next week, so now I'm just going to lie

Repeatedly saying 'I can't even remember the last time I went away', despite it being the exact same two weeks last year … to the same place

Never feeling more
annoyed than when
you've just put in
a fresh bin bag
before leaving for a
fortnight and then
someone eats a
banana ...

Quickly logging in to choose your
seat ten seconds after online
check-in opens to find the only
available option is an emergency
fold-down seat in the lavatory

2. TO THE AIRPORT!

Finding it physically impossible to leave the house without first patting your top pocket, saying 'right, got everything, let's go'

Never being more panicked than when someone says 'taxi's outside!', despite the fact you've been sitting ready by the door with your cases since 2 a.m.

Train due: 05:30
Train expected: 05:35
Time now: 05:39
Status: On Time

Realising, after a two-hour drive, that you actually live closer to your departure terminal than the airport's long-term parking facilities

The pressure to quickly enter your Gatwick Express booking reference (RNZØ3UÜ0y066æ) at the one working ticket machine

Taking a wrong option out of the twenty-four different airport motorway signs offered to you and ending up in a pub car park by the coast

Getting to the airport in time for a quick beer before breakfast, despite your flight departing at 3 p.m.

Staring furiously at the man who hasn't kicked his case another foot forward within seconds of the queue shuffling towards the check-in desk

The indescribable thrill of sitting at the front of the inter-terminal driverless transit train

Being unable to go through a metal
detector without putting on a bit of
a march

Paying an extra £10 to go through the boarding gate first, to then get on a bus with the rest of the passengers

Describing any departure zone with more than three people in it as 'absolute chaos'

Worrying you'll suffocate everyone on board due to the seventeen free sprays of different aftershaves you've sampled out of boredom

Keeping your
passport and
boarding pass in the
very last pocket in
your jacket or bag
that you ever think to
check

Attempting to use your own
suitcase as a stool at any given
opportunity, despite having been
sat down for the past two hours
with an eight-hour flight ahead of
you

Being sure to shred your hands to pieces attempting to rip a freshly bought SD card from its plastic casing, which has edges sharper than a Stanley knife when finally penetrated

Removing a T-shirt and a pair of boxer shorts from your bag and saying 'how about now?' when told your luggage exceeds weight restrictions by 15 kg

Hoping that wearing a blazer and standing up straight will be the perfect storm needed for you to be upgraded to first class

'Sorry, is someone sitting here?'
Translation: Unless this is a person
who looks remarkably like a bag, I
suggest you move it

Feeling the need to mumble
the gate number to yourself the
second it appears on the boards

Hoping the big envelope full of tea bags
doesn't resemble anything dodgy as it goes
through the X-ray machine, in case they
take it away

Forgetting to print your boarding
card, so being contractually obliged
to buy the airline a new printer
from Dixons Travel complete with a
year's supply of ink

3. THE VERY BRITISH PACKING LIST

No Brit should ever travel without these items in their suitcase

Flu capsules

Paracetamol and decongestants are essential, seeing as you will develop a severe cold the second you set your out-of-office email and another one the second you step off the plane on your return

Running shoes

You know you won't use them, it's just fun to fill up half your case with something that'll cover your best shirts in old mud and make everything smell of feet

Factor 5000 sun lotion

The sun doesn't like you, it wants to fry you like an egg. An egg that it hates. Don't give it the satisfaction by smothering factor 5000 everywhere, remembering the back of your legs so you don't spend the holiday walking around like you need a poo

Socks

Lots and lots of smart black socks, because you don't want to walking around the pool with your ankles out like some kind of barbarian, do you?

Sunglasses

Not your expensive designer ones – they were of course ripped apart by a toddler within one day of purchase – but the £5 counterfeit 'Ray-Bams' you bought in 1998, which have never had so much as a scratch

Ear plugs

Like on every holiday you've ever had, the hotel will of course put you in the room that shares a wall with Europe's largest night club, so take ear plugs to use until you finally get the courage to ask to be moved on the fourth night of your stay

Tea bags, Marmite, Wine Gums

Obviously...

A terrible thriller

Anything thicker than a Bible with a title like *Time to Fear*, *Prey to Kill* or *Dead Face Talking* will do the trick, and should be abandoned – greasy and tattered – before your return, freeing up space for ...

Megaphone

A lot of people aren't going to respect queuing etiquette in the manner to which you're accustomed, so use this to send a supersonic boom of tuts their way

Empty space for your return

Four-hundred Marlboro Lights for Wheezy Jim from work, a giant Toblerone, a couple of Milka chocolate bars, a giant Chuppa Chup lolly and those lovely towels the hotel appeared to leave for you in the bathroom

4. COME FLY WITH ME

Approaching a bus with wings cellotaped on and suddenly realising why your flights were so cheap

Declaring for the seventh holiday in a row that you think it should be called 'Aeroplane Mode', much to what you convince yourself is your family's delight

Communicating to the person in the aisle seat that you need to get out by gently touching the headrest in front of you and whispering 'sorry'

Staring solemnly at the overhead baggage compartment as someone rams your hand luggage to oblivion

Never feeling more annoyed than when
someone standing in the aisle keeps
looking back and forth from their ticket
to the seat number that you know for
certain is yours

Watching in horror as fellow passengers go into the toilet shoe-less

Being offered a mint from the
passenger sitting next to you, then
spending the remainder of the
flight worrying your mouth smells
like a bin

Worrying that if there's anything in the world that best fits the statement 'I think there's a knack to it', it's the huge, complicated emergency door you've been told you're responsible for

Asking for a small gin, a
newspaper and packet of nuts on
a budget airline, in exchange for
half your entire trip's spending
money

Watching in horror as the person in
the aisle seat folds down their tray
and places a laptop on it, meaning
you won't be leaving your seat for
another twelve hours

The quiet shame of being unable to close
the hand luggage compartment as the
whole plane stares at you and your stupid
giant fat bag

Would you like ice?

'Ooh yes please'

We haven't got any

'Lovely, thanks very much'

Paying extra for seats with more leg room
then spending the whole flight feeling
terribly guilty about not being taller

The horror of holding on to the
chair in front's headrest as you
sit back down and accidentally
stroking the hair of the seat's
occupant

Putting the complimentary travel
socks over your regular socks, so
nobody has to witness the fact
that you possess actual feet

Not wanting to take your children
to see the cockpit on a budget
airline, for fear you'll see the pilots
don't have instruments and are
sitting on camping chairs

Feeling very pleased with yourself when you pass the cabin crew's seat belt, seat position and bag-under-the-seat inspection with flying colours

Being amazed that you can pay on card while thirty thousand feet in the sky, yet the machines in your local pub only work when the barman stands on a ladder in the far corner

Returning from the lavatory to find you're stuck behind a slow-moving drinks trolley about eighteen rows from your seat and pretending you're absolutely fine with just chilling in the aisle for a bit

'The landing was a bit bumpy'
Translation: I ripped the arm
rests off in terror

You: Cheers, thanks very much,
take care, bye
Cabin crew: Have a nice holiday
You: Thanks very much, you too!

Stepping out of the plane and feeling
like you've been punched in the face by a
sauna

5. FIRST DAY MISTAKES

Not hanging up your jacket immediately, meaning you have to rock the 'one lapel sticking up' look at dinner

Refusing help with your case before being shown to the stairs that will take you to room 10,008

Hopping in an unlicensed taxi to take you from airport to hotel, and noticing after four hours of driving that you seem to be approaching some kind of border control

Wondering whether to set the bedside fan to 'hot breeze' or 'warm hurricane'

Thinking you will be able to teach an entire country about the benefits of adopting your strict queuing etiquette by glaring angrily at everyone in the nearest McDonalds

Accepting your hotel room through
sheer tiredness, despite being
almost certain that it is in fact an
airing cupboard

Gleefully giving someone the equivalent of £750 in exchange for a small tub of pistachio ice cream

Having absolutely no idea what to do with your arms when someone moves in for a triple-cheek kiss

Stroking a local stray dog and immediately losing all feeling in the left side of your body

Briefly opening the window and letting in fifty mosquitoes, twenty hornets, two King Cobras, a naked man and a wolf

Trusting your guidance to a small map provided by the concierge which has had all the most vital street names obliterated by pink highlighter pen

Falling asleep on a foreign underground train after leaving Le Pub and waking up in what appears to be Russia

Saying sorry to locals for no reason and getting annoyed when they don't say it back

Holding open the door of a busy shop and realising you're going to be standing there until the end of the holiday

'Ooh, you've caught the sun'
Translation: Ooh, you look
like you've been swimming in a
volcano

Using an entire hotel mini shampoo and
body lotion like some crazed Roman
Emperor, without realising that they have
to last you the whole week

Still trusting the bottle of sun
cream you started in 1998

Testing out your new language
skills at the local fish market and
returning to your room with three
tonnes of sardines

Ignoring the advice on not drinking the tap water and ending up having to pay for your bathroom to be incinerated

Lifting a bottle of Orangina out of the mini bar, thereby sending a signal to front desk that €1,000 is to be added to your bill, regardless of the fact you immediately put it down again

Checking your work inbox and seeing a chain of 108 emails with the subject line 'Where were you in today's meeting?!'

Being in a perpetual state of adding/removing a layer

6. ON THE ROAD

Booking a hire car without looking up the model, then on arrival noticing the number plate you're looking for appears to be attached to some sort of ancient tractor

Trying to quickly work out who has the right of way: you or the automatic, driverless tram

The emotional roller-coaster of finally finding an empty parking space only to discover there's (always) a Fiat Punto lurking in it

Touching your bare arm on the metal bit of the seatbelt and branding yourself with what looks like a robot's member

Thinking that choosing a classic
convertible in which to cross the
Alps might have been rash, as you
slide gently into a crevasse

Feeling like you're in a film when hailing a yellow cab, until someone steals it and you apologise to nobody in particular

Entering your hire car and feeling as if you've just climbed into the centre of a freshly baked apple pie, despite the scrap of corrugated card you put in the windscreen

Wondering why fellow motorists are beeping, looking scared and entering ditches as you zoom along merrily in the left-hand lane

Leaving your shopping in a hot car
and returning to find your wine has
mulled itself and your deodorant
has exploded

Leaving your shopping in a
freezing car and returning to find
your wine is now an ice-lolly and
your beer has exploded

Starting to regret your decision
to drive your family across
America after you hear, for the
six-thousandth time, 'I spy with
my little eye, something beginning
wiiiiiiiiiiiiiiiith ...'

Closing your eyes and just hoping for the best when approaching the Arc de Triomphe roundabout

Spending a full two weeks bashing your
left hand into the driver's door while
reaching for the gear stick

After driving in a straight line at 55 mph for a couple of thousand miles, starting to suspect there are fewer kicks on Route 66 than the song would have you believe

Never failing to pull up to the wrong toll booth

Being sure the mountain goat is laughing at you as you attempt to manoeuvre your Renault Clio up the 90 degree back road to your villa

Wondering which of the hundred thousand identical parking spaces at the US mall will be easiest to find once you've finished your shopping

Noticing you're about to run out of petrol and regretting the decision to get in the car wearing just your Speedos

Opening the glove box to discover
your stash of Mars Bars are now
liquid

**Worrying you're going to be
arrested as you present your
perfectly valid passport at border
control**

Thinking 'well that's not how I'd have
done it' as the taxi driver throws your
suitcase on top of your camera bag

Soon realising it would be easier
to drive in hooves than it would in
flip-flops

7. VERY BRITISH HOTEL HANDBOOK

Follow these ten simple rules for an adequate experience

1. Check-in

'Sorry, I've booked a room for tonight?'
    'Certainly, under what name, sir?'

'Oh, yes, sorry, under the name … Smith?'

It is vital that you sound suspicious of your own reservation, like a bumbling undercover spy who's forgotten their fake name. You may also be asked 'can I help you?' simultaneously by two reception staff, in which case you should flap around while chuckling in a bid to make it seem like you're choosing left or right on a mental toss of a coin, rather than just the receptionist you find most attractive.

2. Suitable Attire

On entering your room, be sure to unpack straight away. If you have more clothes than coat-hangers the hotel will happily provide more, but this isn't the point, the point is you've packed too many clothes. Who do you think you are? Elton John? Decide which three items of clothing you wish to wear, hang them up and discard the rest. Make a note to travel lighter in future, preferably in one outfit that suits most occasions. Imagine you're James Bond. Or Mr Bean.

3. Toiletries

Keep your toiletries in the bathroom, hidden within your wash bag at all times. Cleaning staff should not be made to negotiate around cans of Right Guard, curls of floss and tubes of fungal foot powder. Similarly, pants must be kept out of sight for the duration of your stay; in order to minimise risk of accidentally leaving a pair on the floor, take them into nearby woods and burn them at the end of each day. Or just wear one pair for your entire stay.

4. Room Service

If you decide to order room service make sure you're presentable when it arrives. Food should not be taken in bed unless you're in hospital, and it should certainly never be taken in the bath. Make sure to stand awkwardly and a bit in the way while your meal is laid out, like you would when the chap comes to read your gas meter. Try to say lots of little 'thank you's during the process, instead of saving them up for one big thanks at the end.

5. Breakfast

Approach the buffet casually – a full-on sprint is bad form. Construct a meal that you'd make at home. Piling your plate with a foot-tall grub mountain is piggish; once you're through the bacon layer, past the cheese layer and heading towards the grapefruit segments hiding under the beans you might feel over-faced. However tempting, do not sneak items for consumption later in the day; it's unbecoming to have a bread roll/tray of bacon slip from your pocket as you stalk through reception.

6. Facilities

Following breakfast you may be inclined to leave the hotel for the day so as not to be in the way, and you should do so, but if you do decide to use the hotel facilities you should abandon any thoughts towards walking around outside your room in the complimentary white towelling robe. You should only wear this within your bathroom and in the two minutes between the spa's masseuse asking you to transfer from standing to lying under the towel, while they pretend to do something just outside the door.

7. The Spa

When a masseuse has finished rubbing you – during which you should have remained as tense as possible so as not to show off – you'll be given ten minutes alone to relax and get dressed. As soon as they have exited the room you should leap up, dress immediately and sit there sweating for the remaining nine minutes. Always feign a feeling of blissful calm when the masseuse re-enters. Then pick up your umbrella and go straight to your room, bypassing the sauna completely.

8. Losing Your Keycard

You've arrived back at the hotel after a night on the sangria when you realise you've left your keycard in the bar. Rather than wake the concierge, it's best to sleep in the car. If this is inconvenient, a good idea is to stand outside the dining room where breakfast will be served the next morning and wait patiently through the night for service to start, thereby bagging yourself the freshest tiny glass of juice and the very hottest egg. If anyone mistakes you for a porter during this time – great! It'll pass the time, you'll get vital exercise and the tips are a great addition to your spending money.

9. Checking Out

Make sure you leave your room just how you found it. Restock the minibar with replacements found at the local newsagents, check for any forgotten items (this will be hard if you lost your light-switch powering key-card on day one and have been living in the dark for three days) and prepare to vacate, at least three hours before you're required to do so. Remember to pick up your wash bag, which you've been using to prop open the door.

10. Saying Goodbye

Thank reception, tell them not to worry about booking you a taxi home and set off on your walk up the A-road searching for one yourself. On arrival home, when attempting to pay the driver, sod's law will have it that you should discover you've left your wallet in the room safe. Then you should suddenly be relieved to find your debit card in your top pocket, but on closer inspection of the card, you'll see the words 'Insert to Unlock'.

'Driver, back to the hotel, please, and don't spare the horses.'

8. SIGHTSEEING SORROWS

Being in a constant state of looking for a
good spot to stop and eat your sandwiches

'Now it's saying we need to be over
there' Translation: I've taken us to
completely the wrong place and I'm
trying to blame the map

Walking around the museum with your hands behind your back, so everyone knows you're appreciating it as much as humanly possible

Mistaking a regular office block for the Empire State Building

Pretending to read the artwork's description while you wait for the people in front of it to go away

Pretending you've finished pretending to read the artwork's description when some else starts reading it next to you

The overpowering urge to buy a bouncy ball from the museum gift shop, despite being thirty-two

'We don't need to go up it, we can see it from here'

Being sure to film hours of HD footage of buildings on your mobile phone, for you to take back home and never, ever watch

'Yeah, could do' Translation: That is a terrible plan, please remain quiet while I quickly think of an alternative

Attempting to just 'nip across the road' in a US city and realising you've made a terrible mistake when you a) get arrested, or b) die

Describing the most important and breathtaking buildings, works of art and natural phenomena as 'not bad'

Sitting in an open-top bus in
the freezing, pouring rain while
stuck in heavy traffic and feeling
pleasantly at home

Being told to 'head four blocks down to 59th and 6th then hang a right' and then thanking the helpful pedestrian despite continuing to have not the slightest clue where you need to go

Using a guidebook that's been in the family since 1973 and realising the country you're reading about doesn't actually exist anymore

Quickly discovering that 'The Latin Quarter' simply means 'The scary old bit that smells strongly of wee'

Visiting some hot springs and immediately wondering where you might be able to buy a hundred thousand tea bags at short notice

The dread of finding yourself as part of an interactive walking tour

Being unable to stop saying 'you call that old?' as you tour the US

Spending most of your holiday
wrestling with a 1:1 scale foldable
map

'Right, let's meet back here by
this hot dog seller in three hours'
Translation: We're never going to
see each other again

Automatically joining long queues
that have nothing to do with you,
eager to show everyone how it's
done

9. TO THE BEACH!

Wondering whether you've gone overboard in bringing a camping stove with you

Removing your T-shirt for the first time in six months and discovering your body resembles a large sack of mashed potato

The indignity of: Trying to balance on an inflatable armchair

Feeling quite annoyed to return
to the same beach as last year
only to find another family are in
'your spot'

Attempting to kick a random
child's football back and both of
you watching sadly as you punt it
into the sea

Wondering where everybody's trunks have
gone ...

Acting like a fighter jet's approaching your face when a frisbee flies within ten feet of your head

Spending so long
attempting to
manually blow up
a crocodile-shaped
lilo that you begin
to hallucinate that
you're having a nice
time

Spending fourteen days attempting to get a rally going with the bat and ball kit you bought when you arrived

The indignity of: Struggling to take your trunks off while holding a towel around your waist

Attempting to wash sand off your feet by standing in a small sink full of wet sand, blasting them with water and then stepping immediately back onto sand

Becoming cross when your child attempts to touch the giant sand castle you've spent the last three hours constructing

Getting sick of everyone saying 'aren't you going to take that jumper off?'

Only being in the middle of saying 'oh, gosh, no, that's quite all right, thank you, I'm fine, honestly' by the time the beach seller has long since walked away

Finding it very uncomfortable when you walk too close to the shore and your socks get wet through

Still managing to find a spot to lie down despite the beach being mostly made up of boulders and tilting at a 45 degree angle

Apologising to the gentleman who's just kicked his beer all over your towel

The overwhelming desire to dig a large hole and sit in it

Wishing you hadn't chosen the big
pink foot-shaped ice-lolly when
you pass an attractive member of
the opposite sex

The indignity of: Flippers

'Ah, this is the life.' Five minutes later: 'What else should we do?'

Attempting to turn off someone's dance music by occasionally glancing at their stereo and quietly muttering 'unbelievable'

10. INTO THE SEA

The overwhelming desire to wear a
captain's hat when aboard any kind
of seafaring vessel

Going into a dive when you've only entered up to knee height, leaving you to scrape yourself further into the water like a tubby crocodile

Taking in two litres of salt water every time you try to say sorry while snorkelling

Thanking a fellow jet skier for what you believe is them letting you pass, despite there being half a mile of ocean between you

Thinking you have the power
to 'shoo' away a massive angry
jellyfish

The exhaustion of trying to look like you're enjoying yourself while attempting to windsurf

The horror: 'Shall we have a go on the banana boat?'

'I think we're in a bit of a pickle'
Translation: We're a thousand
miles from shore, the engine's just
broken, and we've only got half
a ham sandwich and one slice of
Victoria Sponge left

Falling asleep on a lilo and waking
up in a completely different ocean

Assuming the best way to fend off a shark
is to tell it to sod off

Putting on a wetsuit and looking like a large bag of sausages wrapped in cling film

Being amazed to be able to see the
ocean bed through clear blue water,
rather than the darkness and empty
Frazzles packets of back home

'I think I've been bitten by something' Translation: My left leg doesn't appear to be present anymore

Chuckling and saying 'hello, sorry' as you swim past a fellow holidaymaker

The indignity of: Trying to step onto a moored boat

'It's a bit choppy out here' Translation:
I feel like I'm in a washing machine and am really quite fearful for my life

Marvelling at the strange habit of big-bellied middle-aged British chaps who like to get into the sea up to waist height and slowly walk about for half an hour

Trying desperately to look unperturbed when finding yourself floating through an alarmingly warm pocket of water

Apologising to the sea urchin you've just stepped on

Deciding not to risk going in the sea again after being spooked by a floating bit of wood

Feeling extremely self-conscious while doing the mini jog between exiting the water and reaching your family's towel area

'That was nice, you should go in'
Translation: I don't want to be the only person cold, wet and breadcrumbed by salt and sand

11. HOLIDAY BOOZE GUIDE

Name: Sangria
Origin: Spain and Portugal
Taste: Wine gone bad
Serve with: Breakfast
Strength: Varies greatly, from 3–4 per cent (given away to entice you into awful restaurants) to 11–12 per cent (made by you)
Storage: All the ingredients should be kept separately, so you can only ruin your wine when the mood takes you

Name: Ouzo

Origin: Greece and Cyprus

Taste: Anise and regret

Serve with: Fish, olives, feta and an evil grin

Strength: More than three shots and you'll wake in a Greek prison, covered in jellyfish stings wearing only one shoe, which isn't your own

Storage: The very back of your drinks trolley, until your great-grandchildren throw it away

Name: Absinthe
Origin: Switzerland and France
Taste: Like a fist made of aniseed punching you in the throat
Serve with: Caution
Strength: It's ashctually doezzn'ts taschtes tooo bad – hiccup – aster a few schots ... fffbuwtqwobl ...
Storage: Keep well hidden

Name: Tiki Cocktails (such as the Mai Tai and Zombie)
Origin: United States
Taste: Rum and sweets
Serve in: Either a glass or a giant ice-filled treasure chest with six foot straws, whichever is most conveniently at hand
Strength: 'It's an extraordinary concept – you get drunk from the bottom up' – Billy Connolly on the Zombie
Storage: Fridge door, next to the milk

Name: Tequila
Origin: Mexico
Taste: Varies greatly, from 'I think I need a bucket' to 'ooh, that's lovely actually'
Serve: Far away from people who like licking salt off their own body parts
Strength: Half a bottle and you'll end up sobbing that someone stole your sombrero, despite never having one in the first place
Storage: Desk drawer

Name: Jägermeister
Origin: Germany
Taste: Very old chesty cough syrup
Serve with: An energy drink (a 'Jägerbomb') while saying 'oh God, really?!' as it's being handed to you
Strength: After two you'll buy a Jägerbomb for everyone at the bar and wake up with a receipt for £500
Storage: Next to your bank statement with a note saying 'look what it did last time'

Name: Aquavit
Origin: Scandinavia
Taste: Warming (the first sip should make you feel like a radiator)
Serve in: Tulip-shaped glasses or shot glasses, while naked and running through snow towards a jacuzzi
Strength: Strong enough to make you think you're actually enjoying pickled fish as your first meal of the day
Storage: Next to the ouzo

Name: Gin

Origin: Britain (some say Dutch, but we'll ignore that)

Taste: Happiness and joy! (Then sadness)

Serve in: The family's best crystal with tonic, ice, lemon, lime or cucumber, in a deckchair on your staycation (see Chapter 21)

Strength: 'You have to be really careful with it. You also have to be forty-five, female and sitting on a stair. Gin isn't really a drink, it's more of a mascara thinner' – Dylan Moran

Storage: In the cellar with the other six cases

12. DINING DILEMMAS

The horror of tapas: 'How about we just order a bit of everything and share?'

Failing to grab a waiter's attention after saying 'excuse me' twice, meaning you must abandon all hope of interaction and move to another establishment

Always remembering too late that a giant pretzel on a hot day isn't the best idea, as it sucks every last bit of moisture from your body

'Anywhere's fine by me'
Translation: It won't be my
fault when lunch is inevitably
disappointing

Paying €50 for some old rice served on a
burnt pan, masquerading under the name
'paella'

**Going out for dinner at a time
when the locals are halfway
through their lunch**

Having such a bad experience that you leave a four-star review on TripAdvisor

'Can I have a taste of yours?' Translation: Mine tastes like feet

Learning the translation for 'can I have the bill, please?', yet still just mouthing it while doing the frantic 'signing your own hand' mime

'Does it come with chips?' Translation: It had better come with chips

'I'm not too sure about that'
Translation: It's possibly the worst
thing I've ever tasted

Suspecting the restaurant is only for locals as you're ushered to a table in a private dining room complete with washing machine and tumble dryer

Not realising snails were going to taste quite so ... snaily

Asking for a side order of chips with your burger and receiving a large bowl of what appear to be crisps

Returning to a restaurant you went
to during your honeymoon and being
disappointed to find the milkshake
machine is broken and the quarter
pounders seem to have shrunk

Attracting a waiter's attention by apologising to them

Ordering your steak rare in France
and receiving one that's still in its
packet

Ignoring the American waiter's warning that the steak you've ordered is 'quite big' then receiving an entire cow

'Hello, room service'
'Oh, hello, is it all
right to order some
food to my room?'

When your main course isn't what you expected: 'Oh, no it's not what I thought but it's still amazing ... lovely ... different though ... still very nice ... but ... OH GOD I'M SO UPSET'

Saying 'hello, table for deux?' while holding two fingers up: well done, you've been a massive help

Being alarmed when you appear to be served the exact plate of food that was photographed for the menu

13. CRUISE SHIP CALAMITIES

'We've decided to go on a cruise'
Translation: We've done everything
else there is to do in life

Making a mental note to stop mentioning
the Titanic quite so often in communal
areas

Trying to choose between accepting
another couple's dinner invitation
or swimming the 1,056 miles back
to shore.

Famous last words: 'I'm just going for a quick dip'

Looking forward to a break from reality singing contests, then finding half the acts performing in the main dining room

Being the youngest passenger on board, despite being sixty-four

Getting accused of being a skinflint because the cruise you've booked is full of cars and only lasts ninety minutes

Being alarmed that the captain
doesn't look anything like Captain
Birdseye

Opening the curtains to discover your view is of a brick wall ... and wondering how that's even possible

Using the rowing machine in the on-board gym and imagining you're powering the whole ship

Silently questioning the freshness of a salad bar on a boat that hasn't docked for three weeks

Reacting to accidentally releasing all the life boats into the sea by saying 'whoops'

Thinking you should probably mention the gigantic iceberg you've spotted, but not wanting to cause a fuss

Soon realising – as you stroll around the perfume shops and chain restaurants – that your holiday is a lot like being trapped in a slippery airport for a month

Putting your umbrella up on deck
and being blown into space

Only drinking rum because 'that's what you're meant to do'

'Think I might stay on the boat today, give this stop a miss' Translation: I want to be precisely wherever the other 9,999 people on this boat aren't

Knowing that the steak in the restaurant is fresh because your room is down on the cow deck

'I'm fine, honestly, something just went down the wrong way' Translation: I have accidentally let off a distress flare into my mouth

'The boat had rock climbing, wave riding, extreme Frisbee, four theatres and two night clubs!' Translation: I sat quietly in my room and watched telly

Ordering the captain to turn back mid-Atlantic because you forgot to pack Marmite

Being unable to fit your life jacket over your dressing gown

14. BRITS ABROAD: TV, MUSIC AND FILM

I: What are you doing?

Withnail: Sitting down to enjoy my holiday

I: Right, now we're going to have to approach this sci-entifically. First thing we've got to do is get this fire alight, then we split into two fact finding groups. I'll deal with the water and the plumbings, you check the fuel and wood situation.

[A little later Withnail re-enters the cottage from a rather wet and windy night. He is holding a small stick.]

I: What's that?

Withnail: The fuel and wood situation.

Withnail & I, 1987, Bruce Robinson

'I think it's clever how Rome have kept a load of old stuff. There's no overheads, yet people are going over there to see it.'

3 Minute Wonder, Karl Pilkington, 2006

Del Boy: I've done it Rodney, done it. I've booked our holiday. Here you are, my boy. That's it, there it is all in there. We're going somewhere different, we are away from the tourists.
Rodney: Yeah? Where?
Del: Benidorm!

'It Never Rains . . .', *Only Fools and Horses*, 1982, John Sullivan

'Bloody hell. I'm sweating here. Roasting. Boiling. Baking. Sweltering. It's like a sauna. A furnace. You can fry an egg on my stomach. It's ridiculous. Tremendous. Fan-tastic.'

Ray Winstone as Gal in *Sexy Beast*, 2000,
Louis Mellis, David Scinto

Hannah Earnshaw, twenty-three, one of the British hopefuls for a one-way mission to Mars:

'It's going to be challenging leaving Earth and not coming back.'

The Times, 18 February 2015

'When English people go away they recognise each other very easily, you know, they go to France or Spain or Italy and blend into the environment, you'd never know they were there. They sit there enjoying the atmosphere, talking to the waiters ... saying "what do you mean there's no f**king chips? I come here on a plane ... I got children here, what am I supposed to do with that tomato fiasco?"'

Dylan Moran, *Monster*, 2004

'My experience in Amsterdam is that cyclists ride where the hell they like and aim in a state of rage at all pedestrians while ringing their bell loudly, the concept of avoiding people being foreign to them. My dream holiday would be a) a ticket to Amsterdam b) immunity from prosecution and c) a baseball bat.'

Sir Terry Pratchett

'I did not fully understand the dread term 'terminal illness' until I saw Heathrow for myself'

Dennis Potter, 1978

'It … is … terrifying. You're wondering where it all comes from! You start to panic, you think "I'm gonna empty. I'm going to end up a costume of a man. They're gonna find me hung up on the back of the door!"'

Micky Flanagan, on getting a dicky tummy abroad, 'Out Out' tour, 2010

Will: First stop, the Minoan palace in Knossos!
Jay: We haven't come half way round the world to look at some Greek ruins.
Neil: Yeah, you can see that s**t anywhere ...

The Inbetweeners Movie, 2011,
Iain Morris, Damon Beesley

'I'm embarrassed when I see Brits abroad. They have their tops off, wear flip flops and shout at the top of their voices.'

Noel Gallagher

'This bloke next to me, on the plane for four hours ... his breath! His breath! I mean, it was interfering with radio waves! Please face the other way ... you are melting my face!'

Lee Evans, 1995

'There is probably no more obnoxious class of citizen, taken end for end, than the returning vacationist.'

Robert Benchley

'Any man who can hitch the length and breadth of the galaxy, rough it, slum it, struggle against terrible odds, win through, and still knows where his towel is, is clearly a man to be reckoned with.'

The Hitchhikers Guide to the Galaxy,
Douglas Adams, 1978

Mr. Hamilton: You know something, fella? If this was back in the States, I wouldn't board my dog here!
Basil Fawlty: Fussy, is he? Poodle?

'Waldorf Salad' *Fawlty Towers*, 1979,
John Cleese, Connie Booth

'By the time I had finished my coffee and returned to the streets, the rain had temporarily abated, but the streets were full of vast puddles where the drains where unable to cope with the volume of water. Correct me if I'm wrong, but you would think that if one nation ought by now to have mastered the science of drainage, Britain would be it.'

Notes from a Small Island, Bill Bryson, 1995

'I was so pleased to be getting home, after being hard up for months in a foreign city, that England seemed to me a sort of Paradise. There are, indeed, many things in England that make you glad to get home; bathrooms, armchairs, mint sauce, new potatoes properly cooked, brown bread, marmalade, beer made with veritable hops – they are all splendid ...'

Down and Out in Paris and London,
George Orwell, 1933

I go to Blackpool for my holidays
Sit in the open sunlight

'Autumn Almanac', The Kinks, 1967, Ray Davies

15. SHOPPING SLIP-UPS

Being unable to find crisps that aren't crinkle cut, stale, paprika-flavoured and served in 3 kg bags

The indignity of: Having to do a mime for 'whereabouts is the salt?'

Being able to spot your fellow countrymen in the beer aisle by their lack of shirts, trousers and footwear

Accidentally entering the vodka section of a Russian supermarket and getting lost for six days

Being sent out for essentials and returning with a giant inflatable rubber ring, five hundred Calippos and a €2 bottle of absinthe

Pointing at the wrong thing and watching
in silence as the deli server slices you three
hundred servings of elk tongue

**Looking in every reflective
surface the supermarket has to
offer to check out the tan you've
still not really managed to acquire**

Being amazed to see fruit and veg
that doesn't look like it was made
in a factory and then left to go bad

Wondering why every other packet features a picture of a cartoon crocodile in a baseball cap doing a thumbs-up

Being over excited to see a can of
baked beans 'just like at home'

Taking extreme pride in how French
you sound when you say the word
'hypermarché'

The winner of the 'it just never
tastes the same as it does at home'
award: coleslaw

Asking for cheese that most resembles mild cheddar and being shown to the butter section

Feeling the need to say 'no thanks, I'm fine, thank you' to every single market stall vendor in the city

Having sommelier skills that extend to 'if the wine bottle's got string around it, then it's a good one'

Shop assistant: €20

You: I'll give you 15

Shop assistant: 20

You: 17?

Shop assistant: 20

You: 20?

Shop assistant: Deal

Being unable to pass a souvenir shop
without your children insisting you buy
them £100-worth of bracelets made from
colourful string

Melting things in the supermarket
freezer aisle with the heat coming
off your big red face

**Asking for cheese in an American
supermarket and being directed
to the canned goods aisle**

Wondering how many live lobsters
you can pack in your suitcase
without getting into trouble

'Wow, two hundred cigarettes for €3!'
'But you don't smoke?'
'Yeah ... but they're €3!'

Discovering the Japanese soft drinks you've become rather fond of over the past two weeks are actually 8 per cent proof

Just no: Vegemite

16. COACH TRIP TRIBULATIONS

Turning the overhead air fans to create the sensation of someone breathing in your general direction

Wondering if you'll see your suitcase again as it's thrown into the deep black hole of the bus' nether regions

The inevitable horror: 'Hi, I'm Big John, is anyone sitting here?'

Resting your head on the bus
window, despite the vibrations
causing mild concussion

Only eating crisps on a coach if they're
hidden within a carrier bag and consumed
at a speed of one every thirty seconds

Meeting eyes with someone
travelling on another bus and
quickly pretending to look at every
other thing in the world

Really needing to go in the coach's
toilet but not wanting to ruin
your holiday and have terrible
nightmares for the rest of your life

The indignity of: Being encouraged to
join in with a sing-song

Being given fifteen minutes to have
a stretch and use the service station,
but being back at the bus within
thirty-five seconds in fear that
everyone will leave without you

Attempting to close
a bus window by
staring angrily at it

Managing to reading approximately three words of your newspaper before being remarkably ill into Big John's rucksack

The shameful desire to draw a rudimentary cartoon willy using index finger and window condensation as brush and canvas

Dealing with a child kicking the back of your seat by sitting with your head resting on the seat in front of you

Dilemma when offering a sweet to the person next to you: If they say yes you'll have to continue to chat to them, possibly for days. If they say no they probably think you're a weirdo, possibly for days

Thinking that describing this bus as 'mega' is like describing a piece of wet tissue as 'brilliant'

Thinking your coach actually more closely resembles an elderly, forty-a-day walrus than a whippet or a greyhound

Leaving one earphone out for a
bit, just in case the chatty person
you're sat with isn't quite done
with you

Being amazed that the driver has
managed to navigate across Europe for
forty hours straight, powered entirely by
cigarettes

**The indignity of: Pouring wine
an inch to the left of the paper
cup as the bus navigates a tight
bend**

Dropping something, reaching under the seat to find it and discovering a mythical Narnia-esque land constructed entirely from chewing gum

Wishing you'd spent an extra
£10 to get a direct flight as you
reach the forty-sixth hour on the
motorway

Forgetting to thank the driver upon
disembarking and wondering how
you're going to live with yourself

17. CARRY ON CAMPING

Being slightly concerned about just how many human bones there seem to be in the remote area where you've pitched your tent

The feeling of dread as you approach the campsite and only then remembering that last year you said you'd never, ever, do this again

Immediately assigning yourself the vital job of slashing at vegetation with a big knife

On realising you've forgotten to pack one small item
'I'm sure it'll be fine.' Translation: I fully expect the situation to deteriorate rapidly

Watching someone exiting the
Portaloo looking as if they're
the sole survivor climbing from
the wreckage of a terrible plane
crash ... and thinking you'll
probably leave it for now

Thinking you're Bear Grylls because you cooked some beans on the campfire

The thrill of being the first person in the campsite to say: 'I think I just felt a spot of rain'

Responding to the drunk man who has just collapsed on your tent by politely shouting 'Oo-ooh! There's someone in here!'

Suspecting you've set up camp in a bad spot, as your legs are sucked under a combine harvester

Being sure to stop for a few minutes in order to pretend to read any sign telling you about all the types of bird in the area

Waking up to find you've accidentally used a now-quite-flat multipack of crisps as a pillow

'Did anyone remember to bring the torch?' Translation: I'm afraid I've forgotten the torch

Not washing or going to the toilet for a week because the doors on the campsite facilities start at the groin and end at the navel

The indignity of: Trying to put on jeans while fully horizontal

Discovering that a grizzly bear has entered your tent and immediately throwing yourself in front of the biscuits

'Did you hear that? I think it might be a bear!' Translation: I just parped myself awake

Describing having to secure your tent to a 90 degree mountain face as 'a bit hairy'

The indignity of: Carrying loo roll from tent to toilet

Telling your fellow camper that you don't want to hear them play their guitar by saying 'yes that would be lovely!'

'Shall we have a cup of tea?'
[3 hours later]
'I think it's starting to boil . . .'

'Aaaah, this is the life'
Translation: I wish I was in a hotel

18. EXTREME BRITS ABROAD: SURVIVAL TALES

Enjoy these extraordinary tales of pluck and courage while you float on your lilo

Sir Ranulph Fiennes

In 2000, Sir Ranulph Fiennes attempted walking solo and unsupported to the North Pole, where he was forced to pull his sleds from icy water by hand. Back in the UK, he grew tired of his now severely frostbitten fingers, so purchased a set of fretsaw blades and over five days, which the help of a vice, removed them himself. Sir Ranulph's most recent adventure was running 159 miles for six days in 50 degree heat, which the seventy-one-year-old described to the BBC as 'unpleasant'. Quite.

Lawrence Oates

'I am just going outside and may be some time.' According to the diary of Robert Falcon Scott, who led the ill-fated Terra Nova Expedition in the Antarctic (1910–1913), these were the last words of Lawrence Oates. Born in Putney, Oates developed severe gangrene and frostbite on the expedition and, it's said, decided to walk out of his tent into a minus 40 degree blizzard for the good of his team. Scott wrote: 'We knew that poor Oates was walking to his death ... we knew it was the act of a brave man and an English gentleman.'

Bear Grylls

In 1996, in his early twenties while serving in the army, Bear Grylls was involved in a parachuting accident in Zambia. His canopy ripped at 4,900 feet, and he landed on his back, crushing three vertebrae. It was questionable whether he'd walk again, and he spent eighteen months in and out of military rehab. So what did he manage to do in 1998? Become one of the youngest people to climb Mount Everest. Not bad at all.

David Livingstone

Scottish explorer David Livingstone returned to Africa in 1866 to seek the source of the River Nile. He disappeared for years, eventually found by Henry Morton Stanley of the New York Herald in 1871 ('Dr Livingstone, I presume?'). Despite becoming very ill from malaria and dysentary, he was determined to continue his mission, but he finally succumbed to his ailing health aged sixty in 1873; before which he wrote: 'It is not all pleasure, this exploration.'

Maurice and Maralyn Bailey

Not quite as well-known as the adventurers above and below, this couple swapped their house in Derby for a yacht – the Auralyn – and in 1973 set out to sail from England bound for New Zealand. Unfortunately a whale struck Auralyn, leaving the couple in a lifeboat so small they couldn't lie down ... for four months. They survived by eating turtles, drinking rain and pumping air into the raft every half an hour. They were picked up after drifting 1,500 miles, having lost a quarter of their bodyweight during their months at sea. The following year they set sail in their new yacht, Auralyn II.

Rosie Swale-Pope

Wondering if you should take your running shoes on holiday? Rosie Swale-Pope took it one step further than that, deciding in 2002 to run around the world for charity. Setting off from her home in Tenby on her fifty-seventh birthday in 2003, she ran around the northern hemisphere, getting frostbite, broken ribs and a cracked hip as she went, jogging through countries such as Russia, Canada, Greenland, Iceland and Scotland. She arrived home, after 19,900 miles, in summer of 2008 and wrote a book: *Just a Little Run Around the World*.

Freddie Spencer Chapman

British Army Officer Frederick 'Freddie' Spencer Chapman spent three and a half years of WWII in the jungles of Japanese-occupied Malaya. In just two weeks he and two colleagues blew up fifteen railway bridges, derailed seven trains and destroyed forty motor vehicles. The Japanese command believed his work to be that of two hundred commandos. Although wounded, constantly under attack and dealing with bouts of fever, pneumonia and malaria (once unconscious for seventeen days), he still found time for taking notes on birdlife and sending seeds back to Kew Gardens.

James Ketchell

In 2007, James Ketchell had a motorcycle accident which shattered his ankle. He was told he would never walk normally again. Seven years later, he became the first man to complete all three feats of climbing Everest (taking six weeks), rowing the Atlantic (3,000 miles, single-handedly) and cycling around the world (18,000 miles, 20 countries, 214 days). 'After my accident, I felt I needed to do something to prove to myself that I'm all right,' he told the *Daily Mail*. 'I think I've done that now.'

Ernest Shackleton

When the ship Endurance, carrying twenty-eight crew members, became trapped in ice during the Imperial Trans-Antarctic Expedition, Ernest Shackleton and five crew decided to take a 720-nautical-mile journey across Antarctic seas with sixty foot waves on an open-topped twenty foot lifeboat to get help. Oh, and he'd just given away his mittens to someone who'd lost theirs. Upon reaching land, he then travelled thirty-two miles across mountainous land to reach a whaling station. A whaler was sent to save the remaining twenty-two men, four and a half months after Shackleton went for help.

19. COLD WEATHER WOES

Realising that you have to get up earlier
for skiing each morning than you do for
work

Attempting to hold a chair lift for
someone and being dragged slowly
off the mountain

Spending the whole week saying 'who's bloody idea was this anyway?' to your partner, who wanted to go to the beach

Telling everyone you're just going for the Après-ski, as if it's the best joke ever

Having no idea what to do or say when the instructor asks 'how do those feel?' about your skis

Describing the view from the top of Mount Everest as 'really nice'

Being conscious that everyone
else looks like professional skiers,
whereas your second-hand suit
makes you look like you've come to
fix a boiler

Being so excited when you finally master
the nursery slope that you consider high-
fiving someone, before thinking better of
it

**Accepting the first suit the rental
place gives you, despite it being
so tight that people can see your
belly button**

Famous last words: 'I don't
understand, according to the
satnav the lake's meant to be right
here ...'

'Why don't you just ask someone?'
Translation: We've been lost on this
mountain for five weeks now

Quietly hoping that a warm cloth
and some TCP will heal your
shattered fibula

**Famous last words: 'Why on
earth would I need sun cream?
It's snowing!'**

Trying desperately to think back to your training on the Milton Keynes dry slopes as you're falling a thousand metres into an icy crevasse

Seeing another human for the first time towards the end of a three month long mountain expedition and wondering if you should say hello

Soon realising that, no matter what the cost, every ski holiday is basically just Butlins with snow

Concentrating very hard on looking like you understand what the ski instructor is saying, before gently sliding off into a tree

Noticing an avalanche heading
your way and hoping your
umbrella's up to the job

Not admitting that your favourite
part of your holiday was sitting
still and breathing heavily on the
ski lift

**Apologising every time you fall
over and break a limb**

Wondering how much like your Dad
you'll sound if you say 'We'll be going
back to work for a rest after this!'

Knowing you've never looked less attractive to the opposite sex than when attempting to walk across wood flooring on skis

The disappointment: I'm afraid we don't do fondue any more, but there is a full range of cold fish if you'd prefer?

20. HEALTH HAZARDS

Famous last words: 'I'm pretty sure
you don't have to cook this type of
sausage'

Getting a little worried when
you notice the doctor you've
taken your child to has a medical
certificate from 'London's Great
Almond Street Hospital'

Trying to explain to the doctor that you've only been drinking beer because you were warned not to drink the water, but having a rather tricky time forming sentences

Famous last words: 'I'm pretty sure they only rattle if they're having a nice time'

Having to go to A&E in Australia because a house spider punched you in the face

Wishing you'd bought travel insurance when halfway through your cliff dive into twelve inches of sea

The sorrow of finding out that giant hornets love nothing more than the smell of your mosquito repellent

Worrying you've developed heatstroke because you've been outside in over 12 degree heat

Famous last words: 'I'm pretty sure he said drink the water but just don't wash in it ... or was it the other way round?'

Doctor: Comment allez-vous?
Brit: Bien, merci, et vous?

Brit 1: I've been bitten by a snake!

Brit 2: Where? I'll suck out the poison!

Brit 1: On my bottom

Brit 2: I'm sure you'll be fine …

Knowing you could go on holiday
to the Moon and hay fever would
still track you down

Being unable to concentrate on the pharmacist's instructions because you're so focused on looking like you're paying attention

Famous last words: 'It'll probably get going again if we pour some of this ouzo on it . . .'

Putting lemon in your hair to make it go blonder and attracting the attention of eight hundred wasps and a large bear

Typing the name of your new,
highly expensive pharmaceuticals
into Google Translate and
discovering you could have just
prescribed yourself 'an orange'

Thinking you should probably drink more
water when your wee is the colour of
Mars

**Receiving a vaccination jab so
large it feels like the doctor's
thrown a javelin into your arse**

Wondering if your travel insurance
covers jumping off the villa roof
and missing the pool by a good six
feet

Being able to buy anything in
the chemist, from crystal meth
to an MRI machine, without any
documentation whatsoever

Always seeing at least one man in the
waiting room who looks like he's slept
under a grill

Famous last words: 'It's gone from
bright red, to yellow, to green and
now black ... so I think that means
it's healing'

21. THE STAYCATION TEST: CHOOSE THE RIGHT ONE FOR YOU

Answer the following questions to make sure you choose the right 'I'm not getting on a bloody plane' holiday for you

1. Would you prefer to stay in:

A: Room number 2784 in a hotel boasting easy access to famous landmarks (only thirty-five minutes via three trains) and a view of another bit of the hotel

B: An old stone cottage which, in August, has the temperature of Narnia and stairs that require the agility of a mountain goat

C: A house where the toaster settings have been perfected over years and the shampoo and conditioner come in large bottles

2. Do you like a bedroom to include:

A: Tiny kettle, tiny safe, tiny fridge, tiny toiletries, huge deafening telephone
B: Slightly damp sheets, moss, a ghost, a ceiling at shoulder height and a large crow
C: All the clothes you own and a view of your garden

3. Do you prefer to pack:

A: A gigantic map, thousands of pounds and a small umbrella for depositing in a taxi
B: Wellies, a wax jacket and a GPS emergency satellite distress signal
C: Your shopping trolley full of crisps

4. Do you like to be connected online:

A: Using free Wi-Fi pending your filling in of a hundred-question online form, asking everything from email address and date of birth to blood type and favourite chemical element
B: For three seconds
C: In every room of the house thanks to super-fast, fibre-optic, mega-power, hyper-bastard broadband

5. What wildlife are you most interested in seeing?

A: Pigeons, rats (apparently everywhere but never actually witnessed) and foxes frantically freeing bin bags of their incarcerated wares
B: Sheep, cows, what you'll say is a Red Kite but probably isn't, and an angry bull that seems to stare straight into your soul and say 'piss off'
C: Your own dog

6. Do you like to travel:

A: In a labyrinth of tunnels deep underground, avoiding eye contact with thousands of fast-moving, tired and angry beasts

B: By foot, down dirt tracks and across acres of grass and mud, being sure to say 'are you sure we're allowed here?' every time you see a farmer running at you

C: Via the magic of television, from a couch, with your David Attenborough DVD boxset

7. Do you like to eat:

A: In a restaurant you end up picking at random from the 18,545 featured on TripAdvisor after five days of intense deliberation (turns out to be a pizza delivery firm)
B: Between the hours of 12.30 p.m. and 1.20 p.m.
C: Standing in front of an open fridge/ over the sink

8. When buying a drink, do you look for:

A: A pint that costs £7.80 or a cocktail served in what appears to be an old jam jar
B: A pint of roughly ripped-up apples (12 per cent) or a glass of chilled white wine from a bottle opened in 2013
C: The Waitrose delivery man, clinking his way up your drive again

9. For breakfast you favour:

A: The choice between a fry up and some segments of melon
B: Whatever you summon the courage to ask for from the local butcher, and those foraged mushrooms that you're hoping won't kill you
C: Last night's pizza

10. What kind of sights would you like to see?

A: Museums, galleries, statues, famous parks, cathedrals, churches, government buildings, ironic beards and a dishevelled mayor on a bicycle
B: An apparently haunted tree, a picture of the pub landlord shaking hands with the Queen Mum and a bronze statue commemorating a small dog that was said to be a real character
C: Sky Sports

11. You find yourself lost. Do you:

A: Ask someone on the tube for advice and startle the hell out of everyone

B: Call for a taxi, only to be told that he's out

C: Regret finishing the whole bottle, as you cry for help from the wardrobe

12. When shopping, do you like to:

A: Head straight to what you already know is the busiest shopping street in Europe and then act dismayed when you encounter a large number of people
B: Discover a small shop called 'Homemade Origins', which only sells little wooden signs saying things like 'Mum's Kitchen' and 'Champagne o'clock!'
C: Log on to Amazon and order a ninety-eight inch telly for your bedroom

13. For nightlife entertainment, do you favour:

A: Going to see a musical or play, followed by dinner and drinks and perhaps a stroll along the river bank
B: Trying to swing a brass ring attached to a piece of string onto a small hook
C: Repeats of QI on Dave

14. When going for a drive, do you prefer:

A: First gear / Twitching between your brake and accelerator pedal as if you're playing the drums / Rage
B: Driving into a ditch so the tractor can get past without muddying its wheels
C: The McDonald's next to the big Tesco, because there's never a queue at the drive-thru and plenty of parking

15. When you finish your staycation, do you like to feel:

A: Tired and skint
B: Tired and bored
C: A real sense of achievement at finally completing *Call of Duty 3*

Mostly A

You want a UK break that empties your bank account, throws culture at you from all angles and leaves you needing another holiday to recover. Enjoy your mini-break in London.

Mostly B

For you it's all about rolling around in hay bales, going blind off the local scrumpy and walking for miles upon miles down B-roads in search of ... well ... anything to do. Enjoy your countryside getaway.

Mostly C

You're basically a little bit tight, love home comforts and can't 'go' unless you're on your own lavatory. Hurrah – you've taken the term 'staycation' extremely literally for the tenth consecutive year. Enjoy your sofa.

22. NIGHTLIFE NIGHTMARES

'You guys head out, I might join you in a bit!' Translation: I'm not leaving the apartment tonight unless it's on fire

Trying to remember the last time you saw an electronic dartboard and a huge inflatable leprechaun in an actual Irish pub

The indignity of: Realising you can't really handle carrying four pints at once when only halfway back to your table

'Let's just take it easy on the first night' Translation: Let's try our absolute best to not wake up in prison

Being told to 'say when' but instead saying 'stop, okay, yep, that's fine, lovely, cheers'

'I know a great cocktail bar!' Translation: I know a place where we can stand in a queue behind a hen party and watch barmen shake ice about for 80 per cent of the evening

'Well this is fun' Translation: I'm having possibly the worst night of my life

Telling people back home with a wry smile 'whatever happens in Vegas, stays in Vegas', despite the fact you only bet $10 and were in pyjamas each night before 11 p.m.

Sticking to the British theme pub, because it's nice and quiet and does proper crisps

Agreeing that Britain would be better if it adopted half pints instead of pints, as you sink sixteen of them

Hoping the wooden beaded necklace
you bought on the beach has fooled
everyone in the club into thinking
you were born in the mid-nineties
rather than the early seventies

'I'll see how I feel' Translation: You have
more chance of seeing a flying giraffe
later than you have of seeing me drinking
sambuca with you later

**Walking through the bar with a
tray of tequila shots, so everyone
knows you're the prat**

'Ooh, that's not at all what I
expected' Translation: This cocktail
is making me very distressed

Rocking up to the local bar at midnight and finding it's still full of families enjoying some ice cream

'Let's stay up until morning and then find somewhere for a fry up' Translation: Let's fall asleep in this club at 4 a.m., get thrown out and be ill in a cafe

Wondering if the bar that does fifty shots for 50p can rustle you up a decent pot of Earl Grey

No beer is ever as large as the one you mime with your hands when requesting a lager on holiday

Finding that the 'free glass of champagne and a shot upon entry' are one and the same thing

Making sure to never let go of the straw in your drink, to let everyone know just how uncomfortable you are in this club

Finding yourself in the middle
of a foam party and being very
pleased you're wearing your best
waterproof jacket

Describing the night as 'banging'
and knowing you haven't pulled it
off the second it's left your lips

Paying €50 to go in a club because you've
been promised a free glass of Sangria

Travelling eight hundred miles for
a stag do to sit in a pub and watch
the football

23. HOME SWEET HOME

Managing to completely lose your tan in
the time between getting off the plane
and leaving the airport

Passing people in the airport
who are just about to go on their
holiday and fighting back the urge
to have a little cry

Spending the next year with a
Euro in your wallet which you'll
keep thinking is a pound when you
desperately need one

**Saying 'anywhere here's fine'
when the taxi is directly outside
your front door**

Planning to stick rigorously to a
Mediterranean diet from now on,
before stuffing your face with KFC
at the first available service station

Unpacking your suitcase over a period of
about six weeks

'Welcome back, bacon that doesn't shatter when you drop it, it's good to see you again'

Realising that you're absolutely shattered from spending the past two weeks in a constant state of pretending to relax

Being ecstatically happy to be facing a two-legs-under-the-duvet situation again, after a fortnight of kickboxing with a thin balled-up sheet

Wondering if the dog will ever stop
leaping at you in delight at your
return

Wondering if the cat will ever
speak to you again

Wondering why the fish is upside
down

'Can you believe it that this time yesterday we were in . . .'

Opening the post: 'Hi valued customer, we noticed you haven't paid your bill, please do so as soon as you get a chance else we might have to destroy your credit rating forever, have a great day'

Trying to recreate eating at the tapas bars of Barcelona by pulling a stool up to the counter in Gregg's

Finding out you owe
the phone company
two million pounds
because you sent
a text a couple of
weeks ago to say
you'd landed safely

Wondering if you'll ever manage to completely rid your bodily creases of sand

Being able to enter your kitchen without having to do battle with a gigantic double-bodied killer wasp-like beast from Hell

The five minutes between exclaiming how brilliant it is to be watching 'normal' telly again and shouting about how much you hate what's on the telly

Being unsure as to why you've brought home quite so much cured meat

Feeling relieved to be safely back inside a jumper

Saying 'Ooh, do you know what I fancy when we get home? Beans on toast' and everyone reacting as if you've just told them the meaning of life

Finally, looking forward to having a proper, decent, well-made cup of ... OH GOD YOU FORGOT TO GET MILK ARRRRGGGGGHHHHHHH!!!

24. BACK TO WORK

The Very British Post-Holiday Catch Up:

You: So, anything happen while I
was away?
The Office: No, not really
<end>

Discovering the printer hasn't had any
paper for two weeks because you've been
away

Opening your computer to see
your boss has at some point
logged in and discovered your
weeks of water-slide park research
(see Chapter 1) in your undeleted
history

Noticing someone else sitting at your desk and wondering if you should just go back home again

The utter despair of discovering
someone's been fiddling with your
chair settings

'Welcome back, you look well!'
Translation: You're all shiny and
appear to have doubled in size

Being fascinated to know how the
weather's been while you were away

Hearing the words 'where was
it you went again?' on the hour
every hour for your first week
back

Really wishing you hadn't just been pretending to work for the last three weeks before your break

Trying to recapture that carefree Mediterranean vibe by having a microwaved ready-meal paella at your desk

Telling your colleagues that you met someone who was 'a bit of a character', thereby revealing that you met the worst person in the world

Being required by British law
to place a huge bag of airport-
purchased communal sweets on top
of the filing cabinet

Changing your computer desktop background from a picture of a tropical island back to 'solid grey'

'Have you been away? You're not very tanned!' Translation: I'm really quite jealous

The indignity of: Discovering someone's opened your Amazon post to reveal a *Hollyoaks* calendar, *The Student Cookbook* and a second-hand copy of *Home Alone 3*

Trying to get away with a linen shirt until extreme self-consciousness causes you to spontaneously dissolve

Being amazed by the number of people who think they're experts on the various coastal regions of Spain

'No no, keep it, honestly, it's fine'
Translation: I'll remember you stole my pen until my dying day

Thrashing your mouse around for five minutes while frowning at it, so everyone knows you're building up to asking for new batteries

The awkwardness of having to reveal you didn't go to a single one of the thirty restaurants your colleague urged you to visit

'Rained, did it? Oh dear, it's been glorious here!'

Booking your next getaway before you've even turned off your out-of-office

25. THE VERY BRITISH HOLIDAY JARGON BUSTER

What everything really means

All-inclusive

Full of drunks

Bed & Breakfast

Like being at home, assuming you share your home with a clingy old couple who can't stand each other

Boutique Hotel

Tiny rooms full of large furniture that the owners don't want in their house

Bumbag

Where you keep your holiday cash if you have no shame

Business Centre

An old computer on a small desk next to reception (always occupied)

'Check out at 11'

Grumpy maid will knock and enter at 8.45 a.m.

Complimentary

Your room costs £300-per-night but we're going to make you think these three biscuits are a generous gift

Direct Flight For Just £12

Direct flight to airport three-hundred
miles from intended destination

Evening Entertainment Schedule

A magician will guess your card and then
you'll be forced to limbo dance

'Famous Bridge'

Just a bridge, really, wouldn't bother

Finding Yourself

Going on holiday for so long that you eventually start enjoying it despite yourself

Gate 56 / 4 minutes

A two-day hike away through twenty-eight miles of tunnels

Gift Shop

Ashtrays-featuring-Spanish-flag
emporium, storage room for fake
Barcelona FC shirts and home for cuddly
stuffed bulls

Half-board

Toast, Cornflakes and stale orange juice
with bits in ... Enjoy

'Hidden Gem'

Empty

Layover

Forty-eight hours looking at perfume

'Legend has it that ...'

Tour guide speak for 'bollocks'

Mini-bar

Slightly chilled gateway to bankruptcy

Nothing to Declare

A small area that makes you feel like
you're on the FBI Most Wanted list

Now Boarding

You'll be able to get on the plane in three
hours

Off The Beaten Track

A two-day climb and a helicopter trip to
the nearest supermarket

Online Check-in

Giving you the disappointment of picking the middle seat before you even get to the airport

Pebble Beach

Huge landfill of rocks that'll make you wish you chose a sand beach, aka an actual beach

Picturesque

The middle of nowhere

Premium Economy

Free glass of juice

Premium Room

Slightly posher kettle and another chair
you'll never use

Priority Boarding

Get on the plane at the same time as non-
priority boarding but make eighty per
cent of the flight hate you

Rich Ecosystem

Lots of crawly/slithery things that want to
put you in a coma

Rainy Season

Like booking a holiday to your shower

Road Trip

The longest commute you'll ever
experience

Rustic Charm

Exposed wires, leaking roof, birds nesting
in the kitchen, slowly slipping into the sea

Sea View

Speck of ocean visible through high-
powered telescope from hotel roof

Self-Catering

A microwave and a drawer containing ten
thousand old forks, none of which you
want to touch

Tanning Oil

Cooking oil

Tea and Coffee Making Facilities

Tiny plastic kettle, one hot chocolate
sachet, a dirty cup and a wooden stick

Television Menu (In-room)

1: CNN
2: BBC World News
3: Eurosports 2
4-65: Nothing at all

Travelling

An extra-long holiday for people who love
talking about themselves

Turn the Bed Down

Pull the sheets down a bit

Vibrant

Above a disco

ACKNOWLEDGEMENTS

Thank you awfully very much to: All the VBP sufferers out there, including those who follow @SoVeryBritish; to super-agent Juliet Mushens and Sarah Manning at The Agency Group; to the hawk-eyed duo of Hannah Boursnell and Rhiannon Smith and all the team at Little, Brown/Sphere. Also big cheers to Andrew Wightman for his wonderful illustrations; to Adam Bunker for his helping hand in writing this book and to my wife Rhiain and all my family. Ta.

Sorry to bother you again . . .

If you would rate this book as either 'not bad' or 'not bad at all' (steady on), may we suggest that you follow @soverybritish on Twitter for more Very British mishaps and misunderstandings?

And if it's not too much trouble, you might also consider joining in by using the hashtag #verybritishproblems.

There's also a plethora of Very British Problems over at Facebook, should you feel inclined to 'like' the page at www.facebook.com/soverybritish

Thanks awfully.